Then and Now

Buildings

Vicki Yates

Heinemann
LIBRARY

www.heinemann.co.uk/library

Visit our website to find out more information about Heinemann Library books.

To order:

☎ Phone 44 (0) 1865 888066

🖹 Send a fax to 44 (0) 1865 314091

🖳 Visit the Heinemann Bookshop at www.heinemann.co.uk/library to browse our catalogue and order online.

First published in Great Britain by Heinemann Library, Halley Court, Jordan Hill, Oxford OX2 8EJ, part of Harcourt Education. Heinemann is a registered trademark of Harcourt Education Ltd.

Editorial: Charlotte Guillain and Vicki Yates
Design: Victoria Bevan, Joanna Hinton-Malivoire and Q2A solutions
Picture research: Ruth Blair and Q2A solutions
Production: Duncan Gilbert

Printed and bound in China by South China Printing Co. Ltd.

ISBN 978 0 431 191836
12 11 10 09 08
10 9 8 7 6 5 4 3 2 1

British Library Cataloguing in Publication Data
Yates, Vicki
Buildings. - (Then and now)
1. Buildings - Juvenile literature 2. Buildings - History - Juvenile literature 3. Work - Social aspects - History - Juvenile literature 4. Work environment - History - Juvenile literature
720
A full catalogue record for this book is available from the British Library.

Acknowledgements
The publishers would like to thank the following for permission to reproduce photographs: AKG-Images pp. **6**, **23**; Alamy p. **8** (Popperfoto); Corbis pp. **4**, **23** (Julie Habel), **9** (Guenter Rossenbach/Zefa), **10**; Istockphoto pp. **13**, **15**; John S. Johnston p. **20** (NYPL); Lewis Wickes Hine p. **22** (NYPL); Library of Congress pp. **18**; Photolibrary.com pp. **19**, **23** (Tony Bee); Shutterstock pp. **7** (Stanislav Khrapov), **11** (Jim Lopes), **14**, **23** (Ewa Walicka), **17** (PSM Photography), **21** (Ulrike Hammerich); Ted Edwards Photography p. **5** (Photographersdirect.com); University Archives, University of Nevada-Reno Library p. **16**; Woodentop Photography p. **12** (photographersdirect.com)

Cover photograph of house reproduced with permission of Corbis (Museum of the City of New York) and tower block reproduced with permission of Getty Images (Stockbyte Silver). Back cover photograph of cottage reproduced with permission of Shutterstock (Ewa Walicka).

Every effort has been made to contact copyright holders of any material reproduced in this book. Any omissions will be rectified in subsequent printings if notice is given to the publishers.

Contents

What are buildings?

Buildings give us shelter.

We live, work, and play in buildings.

Long ago people lived in caves.

Today we make all kinds
of buildings.

How are buildings made?

tool

Long ago people made buildings with tools.

Today people can make buildings
with machines.

Long ago it took a long time to build.

Today it can take a short time
to build.

What are buildings made of?

Long ago people made buildings
with mud, wood, or sticks.

Today people can make buildings with bricks and cement.

thatch

Long ago roofs were made of thatch.

Today roofs are made from tiles.

Different buildings

Long ago most buildings did not have an upstairs.

Today many buildings are tall.

Long ago some buildings had stairs.

escalator

Today some buildings
have escalators.

Let's compare

Long ago buildings were quite different.

Which is better? Then or now?

What is it?

The way we build has changed.
Do you know what these men
are doing?

Answer on p. 24

Picture glossary

 **cave** big hole in the side of a hill or cliff

 **escalator** moving stairway to carry people to another floor in a building

 **shelter** somewhere that keeps you warm and dry

 **thatch** straw or reeds we use to make a roof

Index

Answer to question on p. 22 These men are high in the sky building a skyscraper.

Note to Parents and Teachers
Before reading
Talk about the different kinds of homes people live in: bungalows, terraced houses, semi-detached houses, flats, detached houses, farm houses. Explain that long ago most people lived in small one-storey houses.

After reading
• Ask the children to make a town of different buildings. They could use boxes of varying sizes or construction toys such as Lego. They should make a label for their building and then display it in the classroom.
• If possible take the children on a 'discovery walk' around nearby buildings (or look at the buildings they can see from the playground). Ask them to notice how the buildings are different, how high they are, what they think they are used for. On returning to the classroom discuss what they have seen and make a list of the different buildings. Ask the children to see if they see any different buildings on their way home and add these to the list.